To:

_____

From:

_____

Date:

_____

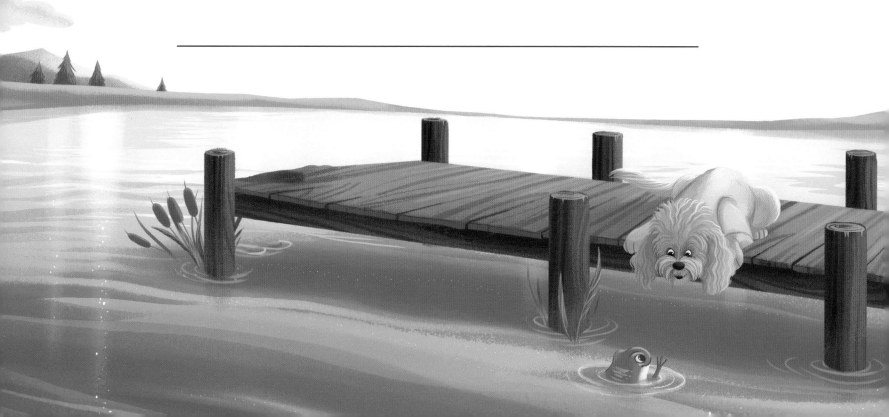

I Can Only Imagine™

A Friendship with Jesus Now and Forever

Bart Millard of MercyMe
with Laura Neutzling
Illustrated by **Sumiti Collina**

An Imprint of Thomas Nelson
thomasnelson.com

Published in Nashville, Tennessee, by Tommy Nelson. Tommy Nelson is an imprint of Thomas Nelson. Thomas Nelson is a registered trademark of HarperCollins Christian Publishing, Inc.

Published in association with the literary agency, WTA Services LLC, Franklin, TN.

Illustrated by Sumiti Collina.

I CAN ONLY IMAGINE is a trademark of MercyMe Music, Inc. Used by permission.

Tommy Nelson titles may be purchased in bulk for educational, business, fund-raising, or sales promotional use. For information, please e-mail SpecialMarkets@ThomasNelson.com.

ISBN-13: 978-1-4003-2133-9

Library of Congress Cataloging-in-Publication Data is on file.

Printed in the United States
18 19 20 21 22 PHX 6 5 4 3 2 1

Mfr: PHX / Hagerstown, Maryland / February 2018 / PO #9471016

I can only imagine what it will be like
When I walk by Your side.
I can only imagine what my eyes will see
When Your face is before me.
I can only imagine . . .

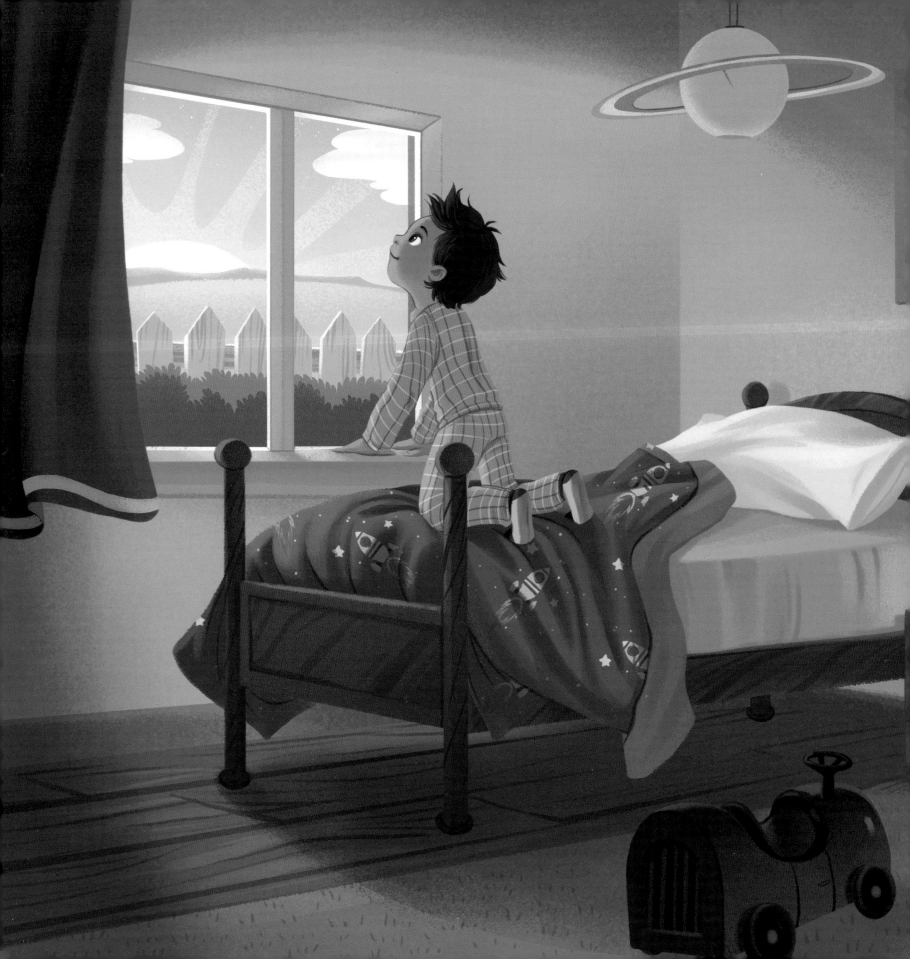

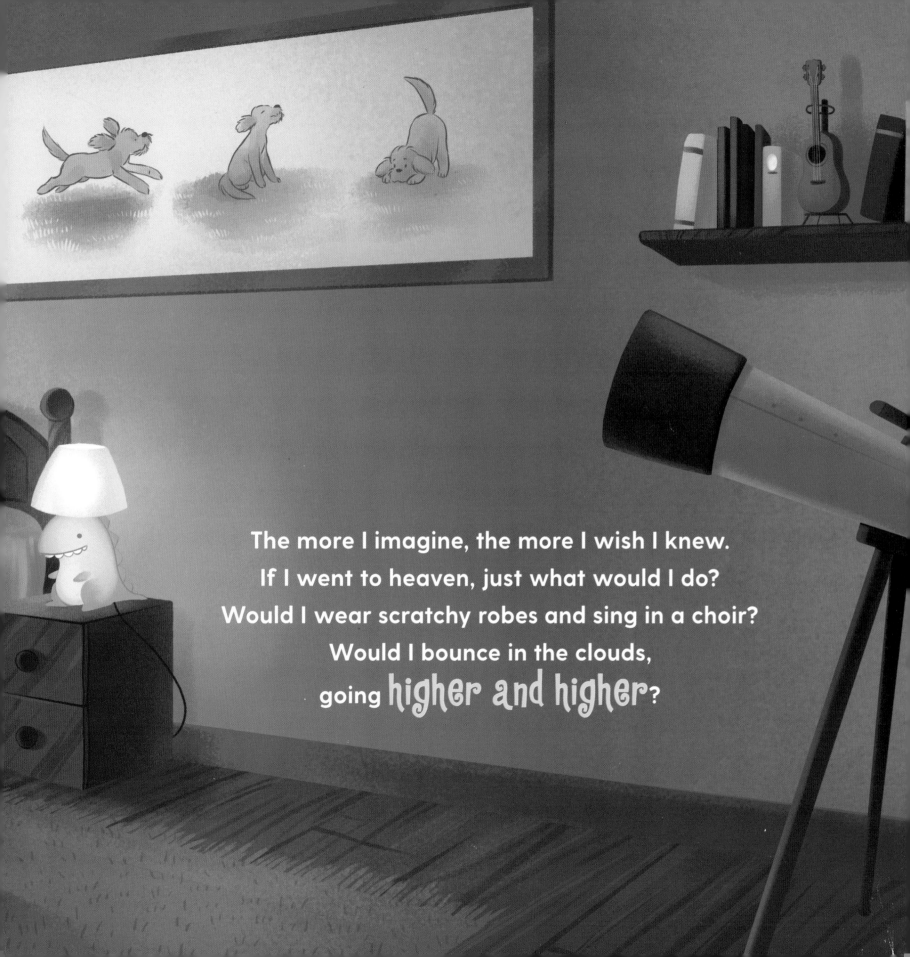

The more I imagine, the more I wish I knew.
If I went to heaven, just what would I do?
Would I wear scratchy robes and sing in a choir?
Would I bounce in the clouds,
going higher and higher?

Do you wake up in heaven
with your hair all a mess?

Must you make up your bed
right before you get dressed?

Is there breakfast in heaven
when your tummy's all rumbly?
Are there fluffy pancakes and
big biscuits so crumbly?

Do the houses in heaven have big rooms and spaces?
Did God **think of me** when He built all those places?

Like basketball courts, a swing, and a slide,
Or a super-cool playhouse with doors on two sides?

The more I **imagine**, the more I wish I **knew**.

If I spent the day with God,
what exactly would we do?

Would Jesus play with me? Would He like what I like?
Would He race with a wagon or ride on a bike?

Would God feel what I feel? Would He see what I see?
Would He like to go on **adventures** with me?

I can only imagine what God thinks is fun.

We could jump in the lake and soak in the sun,

Splishing and splashing and shouting, "Hooray!"

Would God like to float on a warm summer day?

How about ice cream? It's a heavenly treat!
Strawberry swirl is my favorite to eat.

I bet heaven serves ice cream *before* lunch each day,
And the scoops are ginormous, like an ice cream bouquet.

Why, maybe in heaven, God loves to play ball.
Everyone gets chosen. There's room for us all.
Throwing and catching and learning to slide—

When the game's done,
we'd all give high fives!

Surely the **music in heaven** is grand.
We'll sit 'round the fire and make our own band!

The sound is so pretty, we'll all sing along.
I wonder the name of God's favorite song.

What about animals? God made them all,
From soft, fluffy bunnies to crickets so small!
My big dog Lulu's the greatest one yet.
Are puppies His favorite? Does God have a pet?

When I get to heaven, can I sit on God's knee?
We'll all **cuddle up close** and hear His story—
Of how Jesus was born, of His time on Earth.
He'll tell us **He loves us** and show us our worth.

Thank You, dear God, for keeping me close.
Being with You is what I like most.
We know You. We love You. We'll be there together.
Each day will be happy in heaven forever.

I'm sure of one thing that will always be true—
I don't have to wait to spend time with You!
You're **here** in my heart. Your **Spirit** will guide.
You'll never leave me. You'll stay by my side!

I can only imagine what my eyes will see
When we're walking together—Jesus and me.
I can only imagine . . .